TALK IS CHEAP
The Mirror Never Lies

Guide to Making
Student-Athletes
Accountable

GARY McDONALD
With MELODY FORREST

Driven Publishing
Charleston, SC

The information in this book is meant to supplement, not replace, proper baseball training. Like any sport involving speed, equipment, balance and environmental factors, baseball poses some inherent risk. The authors and publisher advise readers to take full responsibility for their safety and know their limits. Before practicing any skills, be sure that your equipment is well maintained, and do not take risks beyond your level of experience, aptitude, training, and comfort.

Printed in the United States of America

First Printing, 2016

ISBN 978-0-9978340-0-0

Driven Publishing

DrivenPublishing.com

Cover Design by Melody Forrest
Edited by Robert Kenney, Thoughtful Editing.

"This book is an excellent resource for student athletes of all ages. It clearly explains the concepts of self accountability, having a plan, and the hard-work it requires to obtain their goals. Lessons learned present the reader with a process to be successful not only in sports but life in general. My son is reading it now!" — Stacey Cooke (Amazon review)

"A lot of wisdom shared in an easy to read book. The guidance offered will applies to any student, athlete or not, baseball or any other sport. I have my soccer player reading it now." — James Logan (Amazon review)

For every parent, teacher and coach that want the next generation of student-athletes to surpass their own accomplishments.

Acknowledgments

This book would not be possible without the love and support of my wife, Kelly, and for that I am truly thankful.

My children, Travis, Kayli, and Ryan, have each played a major role in the book because I have learned so much from seeing their journeys to adulthood and the paths that each has taken. Kelly and I recently started our empty-nest lives together, and I have been reflecting on each of our children's journeys. I remember working with them as the highlights of my life. I hope each reader creates their own lifelong memories as they see their own child reach his or her dreams.

I am forever grateful to all the student-athletes and their families that I have had the pleasure of working with through the years. It has been incredible to watch the highs and the lows and the journey that each of you has taken. My dream is to see these student-athletes achieve goals much greater than I ever imagined for myself. I thank each of you for giving me the courage to write this book.

This book would never have been written without the help of Melody Forrest, her husband, David, and son Scott.

I would also like to thank every coach, teacher, and administrator that I have had the privilege to work with and learn from. Your passion and sacrifice is much appreciated.

CONTENTS

PROLOGUE 11

TO THE READER 13

INTRODUCTION 15

1 ROUTINES.................................... 21

2 WHY? WHAT'S YOUR MOTIVATION?... 31

3 YOUR PATH.................................. 35

4 WHAT MATTERS? 47

5 MISSION STATEMENT 53

6 THE MENTAL SIDE OF LIFE.................... 59

7 THE PHYSICAL SIDE 69

8 BELIEF IN YOURSELF 79

9 CHARACTER 87

10 ROAD BLOCKS AND DETOURS 93

11 CONCLUSION............................. 101

FORM FOR SUCCESS 105

THE GUY IN THE GLASS 113

BIBLIOGRAPHY.............................. 115

ABOUT THE AUTHORS 117

CONTENTS

PREFACE 11

Prologue

I realize that a parent or coach is likely to read this book and ask or demand that it be read by their student-athlete, but please understand, I wrote it for them and, thus, to them. I didn't want to use generalities or even the word *one*, as in "one should follow these steps." I want them to know that, even though they may be exceptional, when it comes to this plan, they are not the exception, and these are the rules.

Feel free to tear out this page and pass along the book to your student-athlete, and if by chance you are the student-athlete, good for you for getting this book on your own. That is exactly the attitude a student-athlete needs to be a scholar-athlete at the college level.

To the reader

Life is give and take. I've made more sacrifices than I can count, from missing social time with my friends to staying up late at night studying. These sacrifices make the rewards even sweeter. Life is about balance. Using your valuable time to be as successful as possible in your life is tough. Life is a grind filled with hard work and sacrifices. At times, I've even doubted my own ability and drive to be successful. I've even strayed from the path of success. I know what it's like to go through the grind and to make the tough choices and the hard sacrifices. Believe me when I say I understand how tough it is sometimes, and trust me when I say it's worth it. Stay on the path. Keep true to your process.

I'll keep it short by telling one story. I'm ten years old at some field in the middle of nowhere in North Carolina, and I'm catching in ninety-five-degree heat. My dad had one rule when I caught, one crazy but simple rule. All I had to do was shake the umpire's hand and introduce myself before the first pitch. Simple enough right? Wrong. I'm ten years old and very shy, so shaking hands with a stranger, especially an adult, was hard for me. So like a typical ten-year-old, I ignored my dad and refused to shake the umpire's hand. What a life-changing decision that was. My parents were furious, absolutely furious. At the time, I couldn't understand why. Hey, it's just shaking someone's hand. What's the big deal? I don't think I've ever run that much in my entire life. I went three for three at the plate, and my parents still made me run.

Looking back, that day changed my life. I didn't realize it then, but I do now. It had nothing to do with baseball. It had everything to do with who they wanted me to be. How I behaved was far more important than how I performed. From then on, I faced my fears and shook every umpire's hand. That made me grow up and interact with adults and become more personable on and off the field. Through baseball, I became a better person off the field and in the classroom. I now have no fear of asking teachers for help, and I'd like to think there isn't a person in the world I wouldn't talk to. I can only thank the game of baseball and my amazing parents for that. As you read this incredible book, don't overlook any minor detail, because you'll never know what will change your life forever. Enjoy!

Ryan McDonald

Introduction

Seeing my son, Ryan, achieve his life's dream is rewarding. Knowing that he earned every accolade is even more so. In the process of learning how to be a top recruit in baseball, my son learned how to work hard and persevere. It has not always been easy for him. He had setbacks and was not always the standout, but he learned the value of focused training, and that skill will serve him his entire life.

When Ryan was born, I was not concerned with whether or not he would be a great baseball player, I just wanted him to be healthy and active. Ryan had medical issues prior to his birth and additional problems the first ten days of his life. My wife and I spent the first ten months of his life not knowing if Ryan had normal brain function. Athletics was the furthest thing from my mind. Looking back, it was a terrifying time in my life, but it put things into perspective: sports are not life, reaching your potential is. And through sports, you can learn the skill of achieving. Do not confuse the two.

Here are two other commands that I will throw out to you:

DO NOT BECOME COMPLACENT.
and
POOR CHOICES WILL DESTROY YOUR
FUTURE!

They sound obvious but are not easy to remember. It is difficult to stay motivated, and every day is filled with multiple choices, most of which are bad.

This book, however, is not about motivation. There are plenty of books out there to motivate you. This book is for the motivated who need a plan. This book gives you steps to achieve your goals . . . even beyond baseball. Learning how to achieve your goals is a skill that will enhance the rest of your life. Everything has a process, and anything worthwhile needs a plan. This is the plan for earning a college scholarship in baseball, if that is the path you choose, but it goes beyond that. It is a way of thinking that will give you the ability to achieve your goals in all aspects of your life.

Before Ryan was a possible MLB draft pick, before he was a college recruit, before he was a high school standout, he was just a boy with a dream. When Ryan was ten years old, he decided he wanted to play college baseball. As his dad, and quite versed in baseball, I did everything I could to help his dream come true, but at one point I realized, even with all my baseball knowledge, Ryan was the one who had to put in the work. I was there for him and answered all his questions, but he had to ask them. He had to evaluate his performance and ask for help. His dream was his, and he was in the driver's seat. I am not saying I didn't have to remind him of his dream from time to time, but my job was to help keep him on track. He was in control of the speed of the train. I guess I should have written *conductor* instead of *driver's seat*, but you know what I mean.

I have learned a great deal more about college recruiting, the ins and outs of skill building, and developing a student-athlete than I knew when I started this journey with my son, and I want to share that knowledge with you. But ultimately, it is still your dream, and you are in the driver's seat. My knowledge will not help you in the least bit if you do not believe in it or follow it. You can try skipping steps, and maybe it will work out for you, but I am 100 percent convinced that these steps are vital for success not only in sports but in life.

At this point, you may not care about the *student* part of *student-athlete*, but at some point you will, and the interesting part of following the process of excellence on the field is you begin to excel in the classroom. This is a natural side effect and, ultimately, is more important because *student* comes first in *student-athlete*.

Follow these steps and see where they lead you, or don't follow them—that will lead you somewhere, too.

"If you raise the bar and compete daily, magical things can and will happen."
—Gary McDonald

1

Routines

Sports. What is it about sports that draw us in? Whether playing or watching, athleticism beyond normal thrills us. The sacrifices that athletes make go beyond the ordinary in order to be extraordinary. Having the privilege to be one of those athletes can be a dream come true.

The irony of the exciting world of sports is that what makes a person a great athlete is repetitive, tedious, and monotonous. The practice stats are seldom as exciting as the game stats, but the practice stats are where the game is won. Winning does not occur on the ball field but in the gym, the practice field, and the mind. Whether the playing field is a baseball diamond, track, swimming pool, or classroom, the winner is determined not by the score or time achieved, but rather by the athlete's ability to master the self-discipline to stick to routines.

Routines sound boring and as humdrum as memorizing your multiplication tables, but routines are the key to excelling in the classroom and on the field. Everyone wants the rewards associated with being a student-athlete, but it takes a complete understanding of routines and the self-discipline to follow through with them to compete daily and excel.

This next statement may be hard to believe, and you may think I am crazy, but here I go: how good you are right now in school and in sports is irrelevant. Yes, you read that correctly. Your current abilities, skill, and knowledge are irrelevant. In other words, your starting point does not matter. It is the finish line that counts. Some may have a longer race than others, but it is during your race that you learn how to accomplish just about anything.

If a student-athlete has peaked academically or athletically in middle school, that is a major concern. There is no glory in reaching your peak in middle school—especially academically. There is too much knowledge still to be gained and too much skill to be achieved. Life is not about how good you are, but rather about how good you can become and how hard you work to get there. Yes, we have limitations, but overcoming them is one of the greatest joys in life and one of the greatest challenges. Learning how to handle challenge will serve you well the rest of your life.

These are mature concepts that some may not fully understand, but if you accept them as fact and follow the process that I am spelling out for you, you will succeed. You will learn how to set goals and work hard to achieve them, and let's face it, baseball or any other sport takes hard work. As a matter of fact, so does anything worthwhile. Hopefully, in the process, you will learn how to enjoy hard work and become addicted and then accustomed to achieving your goals. Don't wait until it is too late. If you delay your focus, you will limit your opportunities. I will discuss that in detail in Chapter 3.

I have boiled down my philosophy into six steps. Though I spell them out here, they are woven throughout the entire process. It is your job to have the discipline, work ethic, and desire to apply these steps. Remember: listen, learn, and apply.

1. **Right now is what matters**. The most important thing in the world is the here and now. If you are in a class, it is what is being taught. If doing a workout, it is the drill. If in a game, it is that pitch. When you learn to focus entirely on the present, you will retain more in school and in baseball.

   To take it a step further, a student-athlete must be able to not dwell on a mistake or get ahead of themselves. On a test, if you do not know the answer to number six, move to number seven, and give number seven your undivided attention. If you are at bat and you have a poor swing or do not like a call, immediately move to the next pitch. The previous pitch is in the past, and you cannot control it.

You must develop the mind-set of giving maximum effort to the here and now. Focus on what process you are doing right now.

2. **The process**. Understanding and creating a process is critical to reaching your peak. You need a plan on how to study, hit a ball, field a grounder, etc. The process uses the correct fundamentals. If you do not know or follow the correct fundamentals, how can you ever reach your peak? If you do not know how to study, are your grades as good as they could be? It is impossible for a student to be consistent if they are not sure of the fundamental rule that they are working with.

If you are working on math and are not 100 percent certain of the order of operations, you will consistently get the answer wrong. The reason for the inconsistency isn't that you do not have the ability. It is because you do not know the rules. The same applies to hitting a baseball. Most young hitters are inconsistent with their swings. Can you write down the correct process (rules) of a proper swing? Can you visualize it? If the brain does not know it, the body cannot repeat it.

3. **Visualization**. The art of visualization is very powerful when it is incorporated daily. After school, it is imperative that you review visually each class that you had that day and preview each class that you will have the next. Mentally review what you did and what you are supposed to do to prepare for the next time you have that class. Make sure your homework and books are packed up prior to going to bed.

   In athletics, review every aspect of your fundamentals, plays, and responsibilities. Visualize the proper throw, swing, bunt, base steal, and cut. Each time you review the proper way of doing something, you are improving your technique and improving your ability to perform in live situations. Again, I cannot emphasize enough the importance of making this part of your daily routine. It is a key element in preparation.

4. **Preparation**. How you prepare for an event will have a huge role in determining the outcome. In school, paying attention in class, doing your work with pride, and studying correctly are all components of preparing for the test. College admissions tests such as the ACT or SAT are nothing more than exams that test how a student has prepared in the classroom over many years. In all sports, you

hear coaches talk about how games are won prior to the teams stepping onto the field. If a player practices and studies poorly, they will most likely perform poorly. Keeping track of your data is an organizing factor and the score card of preparation.

5. **Track the data**. Tracking data is the simple process of measuring your daily work. Whether that be for school or sports, keeping track of where you are helps keep you in the moment, aware of the process, and better able to visualize, which prepares you for the next step. It is vital to be honest with yourself and find an organized way to track your results. It is also important that you make your results public. It is amazing how much harder we work if we know others will learn the results. If you need proof, let me ask you: how much would you care about your grades if you knew your parents would never see them? Enough said.

When you track data, you are in essence competing against your previous results. This is the only way you can compete every day, and the more you become comfortable with competing against yourself, the more you will win and the more winning becomes a habit.

6. **Win the moment.** Every event throughout the day is a moment that you should try to win. In history class, challenge yourself to stay mentally strong and get the most out of what is being taught. For lunch, try to eat a meal that is going to benefit your goal of weight gain, loss, or maintenance. On a test, set a grade goal and challenge yourself to beat that grade. In athletics, try to win every drill, set, or event. The more you compete, the stronger mentally you will become.

There will be many times when you will lose, and that is good. Often we learn more from our so-called losses than from our victories. Use a loss to test your process and preparation. Evaluate what went wrong and improve. If by chance you keep winning, then raise the bar so that it becomes more challenging. For example, if your goal is to get a 92 on tests and you consistently achieve your goal, aim for 95. When you consistently track your data and win the moment, you create a powerful routine.

Success has a price and that price is self-control and the mental discipline to grind this out on a daily basis. Please understand that these routines are not based on how big or strong you are or even how smart. They all require the same thing to be successful: the determination to follow through on a daily basis. Yes, daily.

Your first assignment: get a journal. Find a notebook of some sort that is strictly for this plan. It doesn't have to be fancy. It just has to have one purpose, and that is to keep your thoughts organized.

This is your first assignment. DO NOT SKIP IT!

"No mountain is conquered with short cuts. It takes planning, training, diligence, and most importantly, the heart to not give up."
—Melody Forrest

2

Why? What's your motivation?

Have you ever stopped to ask yourself why you want to be a good student or play college baseball? When setting goals, this step is often missed, and in reality, it may be the most important one. Recognizing your motivation helps you stay on track, and sometimes, knowing the source of that motivation can change your goals.

Every goal deserves a reason. Heading blindly into years of work without knowing your motivation is a waste of time, but oddly enough, many never give it a thought. Why? Because it is difficult to pinpoint a reason. Many times it is just something they have done for years, like a feud that has been going on so long that no one remembers why it started.

What started your dream? Was it the feeling you got when you got a hit? Was it the smile on your parent's face when you showed her an A on a test? Those are both good motivations, and there is nothing wrong with them. Are they yours?

If you are having trouble figuring it out, you are not alone. Sometimes it takes deep reflection to understand your motivation, but once you label it, it will help you stay focused. If you never label it, at some point you will try to rationalize your dream away. What I mean is that you will convince yourself it was never your dream. Don't let that happen. Know your motivation, and accept that you have a dream, a dream that will take much hard work.

Give yourself time to think about it. It may take minutes. It may take days, but give yourself whatever amount of time it takes. You don't have to stop reading in the meantime. You might find the source of your motivation in these pages.

Having a precise definition and reason will help make your dreams a reality. You may have a love for the game and cannot imagine not playing. You may want to get into an Ivy League school and need all As. Sometimes our motivation is based on money; earning a scholarship to help pay for your college education is a great reason. Sometimes it is based on pleasing our parents; making mom and dad proud should never be overlooked, but it can be difficult to stay motivated when the dream is not your own.

You may be one of those people who love a great challenge or feel a desire tugging at your heart. That is fine, but those are the easiest ones to rationalize away. It is so important that you write down words of encouragement to your future self. What I mean is write a letter to yourself, and remind yourself why you started this journey. Later in the book, I will ask you to write a mission statement. Be sure that step is not skipped.

Another motivation that is common is the drive to succeed because no one believes you can do it. This can be powerful motivation. Please ask your future self, "Is this really what I want? Now that I am here, do I want to play college ball?" I am not trying to get you to quit. I just don't want you to make sacrifices for the wrong reason.

Like I said, give yourself some time. Figure out why you want what you want. That way you cannot talk yourself out of your dream when the going gets tough, and believe me, it will.

Now write it in your journal.

"If you don't know what drives you,
how can you stay driven?"
—Melody Forrest

3

Your Path

How far . . . how badly . . .
what are you willing to give up?

This chapter is all about your future. Where do you want to go in life? That is a huge question that many adults never ask themselves. But think about it. If you don't know your destination, how can you plan your path? Realize that where you want to go will determine your path, and if you don't determine your own path, one will be chosen for you by default.

I don't know how old you are or what your goals are, so understand that I am not judging you, but there comes a time in everyone's life when they must judge themselves. I am not asking you to face the limits of your abilities, but rather to think about your work ethic—past, present, and future. Do you honestly feel you have worked as hard as you can at baseball? How about school? Could your grades be higher? Could your knowledge be greater? These questions must be answered before you can start to figure out what post–high school path you want to follow.

I meant it when I wrote that it doesn't matter where you are right now. Understand that you have yet to reach your peak. What I want you to think about right now is: where is your peak? Do you want to play college baseball? Do you want to play for Harvard?

If you are like most students, you get up early during the week and go to school. Why? Why do you go to school? Some will say, "it is illegal not to" and others may say, "because my parents make me." Hopefully, most of you will say, "because I want to learn" or "I want to earn good grades." If you only go to school because you are forced to, you should either reconsider playing college baseball or change your attitude toward school. It takes much more than athletic ability to play college sports—especially baseball.

Consider this: what you are learning right now could affect what college you go to. Does that seem hard to believe? The truth is that every day at school holds a chance to get better grades and learn something for the ACT or SAT tests. Let me explain something about these standardized tests. They are tools to help colleges compare two students from two different high schools. If they only used a student's grade point average (GPA), every student from an easy school or who only took easy classes would be selected over a student who went to a tough high school or took tough classes. The ACT and SAT tests erase any grading advantage of one school over another because they test knowledge. So, if you are going to school to gain knowledge, you may do very well on a standardized test; if you are not, well, I think you get the idea.

So what are the paths for athletics and academics? I boil it down to three different paths for each. There is no right or wrong path, but realize before you chose which path you want to work toward that everything comes at a cost. Success has a cost and so does failure. Are you willing to pay the price? You pay for success up front, and failure has a delayed price tag. Either way, there is a cost. Every day, you have the choice to either make a payment toward success or create a debt that will have to be paid. Read that last sentence again. Let it sink in.

I am not trying to scare you. I am trying to open your eyes to reality. I have no doubt that if you want to become a better student or athlete, you can if you follow the plan that I am teaching you, but first you have to determine your path.

Each person has to do the path that is best for them. Your parents might want you on one path, and you might want to be on another. It is imperative that you discuss your goals with your parents and come to some sort of understanding. Otherwise, it will be very difficult to complete either path.

The three paths of baseball:

- Baseball path 1:
  Baseball is OK. I enjoy playing the games. Practice is all right; I enjoy being with my friends on the field. I don't like training. I am not going to get in front of the mirror and practice my swings, and I am not going to learn a bunch of plays and rules, but I have fun with it. Next season, I will like basketball.

  There is nothing wrong with that path. It is normal, but realize you have very little chance of playing college baseball.

- Baseball path 2:
  I want to play high school baseball and would like to be good at it. I am a good athlete and enjoy playing other sports. I enjoy training and like lifting weights and running, but I probably won't be polished enough to play in college, and that is OK because I don't want to play college sports. I just want to play high school sports, and I don't want to work that hard on sports in college. I want to work hard on my grades.

  There is nothing wrong with that path either. It is a well-focused plan and, frankly, the right choice for most high school athletes. College is important, and giving yourself the best shot at a good education is wise.

- Baseball path 3:

I want to play college baseball. I have a passion for it. I love it, and I want to be a ballplayer. I understand I need to be fundamentally flawless and have a high IQ for the game. I am willing to work at it.

This is the path of most college baseball players, and I am going to assume that this is the path you want to follow. I want you to realize, however, that even with this path, there are levels. The goals you set in order to play baseball for Harvard will be much different than your goals in preparing to play for the University of Florida.

If, by chance, you chose paths #1 or #2, don't stop reading. The steps in this book will help you regardless of your baseball dedication.

The three academic paths:

- Academic path 1:

You struggle in school. You tend to talk when the teacher is talking, and you are there for the socialization. You don't take it seriously, and you get into a little bit of trouble. You are just trying to pass and are thrilled with Bs.

Can you still go to college? Yes. Can you go to Clemson or Harvard? No.

- Academic path 2:

You do well in the classes that you love but not in the classes that you don't. You behave in class, but you only put forth effort when you are motivated.

Can you go to Harvard? No. Clemson? Maybe.

- Academic path 3:

You are self-motivated. You enjoy learning. You understand that you must get good grades no matter what the subject. You pay attention in class, and you don't get caught up in the distractions. You are in school to learn. You like a challenge, and you raise the bar constantly. You are never satisfied with your current stats or grades. "How can I do better" is your way of life.

Can you go to Harvard? Maybe. Clemson? Most likely.

Before you decide on your path, realize that a college education is worth, on average, one million dollars above and beyond the cost of tuition. During your lifetime, if you have a college degree, you will make one million dollars more than a person who does not.

Baseball scholarships are worth about $50,000 per year at a big five conference when you add up all the special privileges you get: doctor's care, nutrition, tutors, equipment, etc. Consider your high school years as the time to earn that money. Tell yourself you are making big money to make good grades, get a high ACT or SAT score, and work really hard at baseball. Tell yourself the same thing when you go to college, except with a large pay raise. One million dollars is a lot of money, but participating in college sports may be worth more than just money. While playing sports, you learn leadership and discipline. You will land a better job if you have athletics on your college resume. Why? Because job recruiters know you have to work hard to achieve goals and compete in sports.

You may have given a lot of thought to what college you would like to play baseball for, but have you considered the academics? Do you know if the college offers the degree you want? Do you know what GPA is required to get in? You cannot wait until your senior year of high school to start concentrating on college. Starting your freshman year, you need to know what grades you need to get into the college of your choice. How terrible to be good enough to play college baseball and not have the grades to get in. On the other hand, why go to a school that isn't the best fit for your academic growth? Most students pick a college because of its location or prestige. Some pick a college because it was the only one they got into. Pick a college that fills your needs.

The key to achieving any goal is learning what is required. If you want to improve your batting stance, you seek knowledge. If you want to ace a test, you study. The same is true for wanting to attend a certain college. You must learn what they require.

You must know what GPA and ACT or SAT scores are necessary, and if you want to play baseball, you must learn what level of athlete the school recruits. You must learn if throwing an eighty-five-mile-an-hour fastball is good enough for the college you want to attend. If you score a 29 on your ACT, you must learn if that is high enough for the college of your choice. Each college will have different requirements, and some will be harder to meet than others.

How do you get into the college of your choice?

You need to prove you are capable of attending that college. You must pass through the series of thresholds that it requires. Think of these as doors, and the more doors you have, the better your chances of finding one that will open.

The first and most important door is your GPA and test scores. If you do not meet the admissions requirements, that door will remain locked no matter how good an athlete you are.

Another door is extracurricular activities. Playing sports in high school is a big plus, but sometimes it takes more than that to show you are well-rounded. Joining school clubs and volunteering may also help you get into the college of your choice.

Let's take this a step further. Let's say a college is interested in you for its baseball program, and it is between you and another recruit. Your GPA or ACT score could be the tiebreaker, or possibly, your participation in after school activities could be the deciding factor. Don't be on the losing end of those tiebreakers.

On a side note, did you know that you can take the ACT up to twelve times, and you can choose which score to send? With SAT Score Choice, you can apply using your best score from each category. So, retake the tests until you are satisfied with your score. Remember: tiebreaker.

Can you change paths?

Think about the paths as levels on a mountain. Path #1 is at the base, path #2 is in the middle, and path #3 is at the top. If you have chosen path #1 and have stayed at the base and later decide to pursue the peak, the climb will be harder than if you had decided on path #3 at the start. It also depends on how much time you have. There comes a time when it is too late to make it to the top—no matter how fast you try to sprint up that mountain, it has become out of reach.

If you are climbing toward path #2 and then decide to go for path #3, you may be able to reach the peak, but it depends on how far away your peak is. You may have to lower your peak—in other words, attend a smaller program—because the top baseball schools begin recruiting after a player's freshman year of high school. If you wait too long, those programs will have already filled their spots, and it will be too late. Regardless of program, time will always be a factor. Make sure you have enough time to reach the goals on your path.

If, however, you have been methodically scaling the mountain on path #3 and you decide to change to path #2, all you have to do is turn around. It is always easier to go down.

You may not know which path you want to pursue, but why not aim for the highest right from the start? Don't limit your options before you make a choice. Raise the bar. Get the greatest grades you can, so when you do decide, you will not be limited by your GPA. The same works in sports. Know what is needed for the best schools and aim for that—beyond that, even. Know what they require, and aim for that peak. When you understand the rules, you are armed with a roadmap to help make you more successful.

I love the saying "Aim for the stars. If you miss, you may hit the moon." That is what these paths are all about. You will never achieve higher than your aim. Aim high. How high is your star?

What have you got to lose?

Your assignment:
- Pick five colleges. Know what GPA is needed to get into each, as well as what ACT or SAT score each requires.

- Learn or figure out your GPA.
- Take the ACT and SAT over and over again until you are satisfied with your score.

So, what's your path? Think about it and then have this important discussion with either a parent or mentor. Whether you want to believe it or not, someone who has lived beyond adolescence has a greater understanding of adulthood than you do. Ask adults if they would have done anything differently, if they have any regrets. And ask what they did right. Listen to them, and understand that choices were made and outcomes were determined. Don't be surprised by cause and effect. Every choice has an outcome, and the only person who can decide what you are going to do each day is you, but that doesn't mean guidance isn't important.

"Only those who will risk going too far can possibly find out how far one can go."

—T.S. Eliot, author

4

What matters?

If you had the choice to play in a tournament or spend three hours doing drills and mirror work, which would you do? Most, if not all of you, would choose the tournament. Playing games is fun. Winning is even more so. Trophies are nice to earn, and bragging rights feed the ego, but do they make you a better ballplayer? Do they measure your ability? No, at most they measure your team's ability compared to another team's, but even that is up for debate, depending on how the teams played on that day and at that time.

Think of baseball games as tests. If all you did in school was take tests, you would learn much less than if you read, filled out worksheets, and studied. Likewise, if all you did was play baseball games, you would learn much less than if you practiced drills, did mirror work, and studied plays. Games should be used as a tool to test your current ability. They are perfect for seeing your progress with the skill set you have been working on. Do not fool yourself into thinking that tournaments will help you become a better baseball player.

Sometimes games can make you a worse player. Falling back on your familiar old technique can hinder progress with your new one. It is difficult to test your new skills when you have an audience and a team is relying on you, but realize that you will never fully embrace the better technique if you are continuing to reinforce the bad. You may strike out, and your team may lose the game, but stay true to your progress. Trust me on that one.

Let's talk about uniforms. I know a high school team that has six uniforms. Six! Though in itself that isn't bad, it is when their batting cages are unusable and their practice field a disgrace. Who cares how many uniforms a team has? Does it matter if they look good while playing poorly?

Some may say it gives the team a sense of unity and confidence. That may be, but confidence can only take you so far. Do you think a pep talk the morning of a test for which you have not studied will make answers magically appear in your head? No. Then why would a uniform magically make you a better player? Uniforms are only important when you have the skill to back them up, and that skill is acquired in batting cages, in front of a mirror, and in the weight room. Earn your uniform. And if by chance you are good enough to earn six, you should be in the pros.

As a side note, did you know that the number one reason most players pick a college to play for is the look of the uniform? Don't be that guy! Pick a program that will help you develop as a player or get you the degree that you desire. That rule applies to all levels of baseball. The uniforms do not matter.

Don't get caught up in the hype of trophies, tournament records, and uniforms. Keep your eye on your own skill set and ways to increase that skill set. Start with the basics. To succeed at baseball, you need to master the basics. Fundamentals are not exciting, but they are vital, and they win games.

There is a quote about playing for the name on the front of the jersey instead of the one on the back. Though I understand the concept of being a team player and not trying to show anyone up, in reality, what you do on the field is a direct reflection of the name on the back of the jersey. The back of the jersey represents who you are and should show how hard you have worked.

So which name should you play for? I say neither. Never sacrifice your health or well-being in order for the team to win a game, and never be a show-off, but be an expert at your position. Do what a first baseman or catcher should do. Be true to your responsibility. If you are a catcher, know your first job is to frame a pitch and your second is to throw out the runner. Realize the name you play for is the third, unwritten name: that of your position. Play for your position— not prestige, recognition, or accolades. Play your position to the best of your ability. Do what you are supposed to do, and do not own what others do. If a player is out of position when you go to throw a ball to second base, throw it anyway. Play your position.

What do you have to do before you can play your position? You have to know it. Study it. Study other players. Study plays and know exactly what your position is supposed to do. Do not worry about if the other players are doing their job. That is the coach's responsibility. Know your position. Practice your position. Visualize plays. Play your position. That is what matters.

Winning trophies: doesn't matter.

Uniforms: nope.

Your skill set: yes.

Knowing your position: absolutely.

Your teammates knowing you know what to do: vital.

"You have to decide what your highest priorities are and have the courage—pleasantly, smilingly, nonapologetically—to say 'no' to other things. And the way to do that is by having a bigger 'yes' burning inside."

—Stephen Covey, author

5

Mission Statement

What's Your Vision?

Have you ever written a mission statement? Do you know what one is? It is a summary of your goals and values and I think it is the secret to staying on task. There is something powerful about a goal that is in writing. Whether it is a to-do list or your life's dream, writing it down increases the possibility of accomplishing it. When you see it in writing, it becomes real.

Trust me when I say you will need this statement to remind you of your goal because there will come a time when you will want to give up. You will have setbacks, and your time will become valuable. You will want to give academics and baseball a back seat to friends and video games. I am not saying you cannot have friends or play games. I am saying you must keep their importance in perspective.

Have you heard the saying "Anything worth doing is worth doing well"? I think it is a very good statement and explains the dedication you need to be a scholar-athlete. In contrast, do you know the saying "Anything not worth doing is not worth doing well"? Think about that statement. Don't you think video games fall into that category? So many kids spend countless hours learning how to play a game with no real value beyond entertainment. Again, entertainment in itself isn't bad, but five-hours-a-day is. Remember that, when you write your mission statement.

You do not have to share this statement with anyone, even though I recommend you do. I do, however, want you to memorize it. You need to see it in your mind's eye when you are working out and you think you cannot do another rep. You will need it when your friends want you to play video games instead of practicing. And you will need it when you don't make the team you were hoping for.

Players have setbacks all the time, and it is the players who don't let those setbacks stop them who succeed. I could write many stories of ballplayers who wanted to quit and went on to greatness, but those stories can be found in many different books.

Find them on your own. Think about the players who didn't quit, when you write your mission statement.

Where do you start when you want to write a mission statement? Start with the end in mind. Remember your path. Visualize it. If you want to play baseball for Harvard, imagine yourself on their field. If you don't know what the field looks like, visit it or look it up online. What if you want to play for the Atlanta Braves? Do the same thing. How does it feel? Write it down. For example: *I want to be a starting pitcher for the Atlanta Braves. I want to experience the sound of the crowd and see my catcher give me signs. I want to hear the umpire yell, "Strike!"* I know it is corny, but it works.

Now go backward. What skills do you need to be on the mound in SunTrust Park? Write them down. Now set goals with steps to get you there. For example: *Throw 68 mph by eighth grade, 75 by sophomore year, 85 as a junior.*

Now let's combine those sports goals with academics. If you want to play for Harvard, you better set grade goals and standardized testing goals. Actually, that is true for any college you want to attend. Realize that the better your grades, the better scholarships you may earn. Do not rely on your athletic ability to get you all the money to attend college. That just does not happen in baseball. Help out the baseball coach by getting a nice academic scholarship. Do that by setting goals and including those goals in your mission statement.

Sometimes inspirational words can help form your mission statement. It can be a quote from a hero, a Bible verse, or even a saying that you have made up. Just make sure it is something that inspires you and reminds you that your goals are important. You could even call it your mantra.

Before you start writing, let me dare you to go big. This is your dream. Don't dream for something easily attainable. Be outrageous. Go beyond your comfort zone. Have the guts to be different and bold. Realize that dreaming big is scary. If it isn't, your dream isn't big enough.

I read the other day that the secret to happiness is to set low standards. I think that is ridiculous. I understand what they are trying to say. If you dream big, you might have to deal with disappointment. Big deal. I say if you don't dream big, you will be disappointed. The secret is to try your hardest and accept the outcome. Don't believe you have total control of your destination. You have control of your thoughts. Make them big. Have fun. Enjoy the outcome knowing you gave it your all. The secret, however, is giving it your all.

Assignment: Come up with your big-dream mission statement and write it down. I also want you to come up with five positive ways that just going for this dream will affect your life. Now try to come up with three negative effects. Hopefully the second part of that exercise will be harder than the first.

"Talk is cheap.
Show me you mean it by writing it down."
—Gary McDonald

6

The Mental Side of Life

When I talk about the mental side of baseball, I am not talking about visualizing plays or studying players. I consider that still the physical side because you are focusing on what the body is doing. The mental side is that part of you that keeps going when you don't want to. Some people call it heart. Some call it tenacity. Call it what you want, but it is the difference between mediocre and great.

In sports, it is the self-discipline to push harder and to not give up. In academics, it isn't the ability to answer questions correctly but rather the courage to say no to friends when you have to study. That is not easy, but it is the difference between achieving your goals and watching them slip away.

Many coaches do not believe that this mental fortitude can be taught. They believe you are either born with it or you are not, and they have determined that a lack of mental toughness is an indication a player should be weeded out of consideration for the next level. I believe that is a bunch of garbage. The mental side of sports is a learned skill like everything else. It takes research and trial and error. It is not one size fits all, but it can be taught, which means it can be learned.

The best description of the mental side of sports is the ability to be a competitor day in and day out. The ability to compete is a valuable skill on the field and in the classroom. To become better, you must learn to compete every single day of the year, and the more you practice this mind-set, the better you get at it. Competition helps focus your mind and fine tune your skills, but be aware of who you are competing against. You are not competing against other players or other students. You are competing against yourself.

If you compete with others, you are both setting yourself up for defeat and limiting your progress, depending on the competition. Do not compete against the strength of someone who is six inches taller and weighs thirty pounds more than you, and also, do not settle for being stronger than someone six inches shorter than you and who weighs thirty pounds less than you do.

You cannot have a better competitor than someone who is exactly your size and exactly at your level. The choices you make will determine the victor—yesterday's you or tomorrow's you. Realize that you are either getting better at something or

60

getting worse. There is no staying the same. If you cannot compete with yourself, you will never learn to compete against others, and you will have a meltdown.

Bad games happen. Meltdowns happen. Everybody's gone through a stretch of lost confidence. This happens at every level. It is your ability to get through this stage and learn from it that matters. The better you become at competing, the better you are at the mental side of everything.

To get better at anything, you must embrace these basic truths:

- Reaching or not reaching a goal does not happen by accident. Your outcome is a direct result of what you do on a daily basis.

- The difference between success and failure is the ability to do what others are not willing to do. Sacrifices must be made. Effort must be expended.

- Go beyond what you think you are capable of. Only when you go beyond your comfort zone will you reach what others only dream about.

- Talk is cheap. What you accomplish is what counts. Actions speak louder than words. Every athlete wants to be a professional, but few are willing to put forth the effort to become one.

- You are only as good as you are today. The past does not matter. You are what you are today. You are as strong as you are today. Forget what you were, and don't expect tomorrow to be better if you do not put in the work and compete with your current self.

If you choose to be a competitor and find a way to improve yourself every day, understand and accept that you won't be doing what everybody else is doing. Can you fight the urge to fit in? Can you resist the pressure to be like them? Following the crowd is easy. Blazing a different trail is difficult. Going with the crowd creates mediocrity. Going with the flow will never create greatness. In the crowd are unrealized dreams and lost opportunities.

Take a look around and see what everyone else is doing. Are they wasting time watching mindless videos or playing video games? Are they spending countless hours on social media? What are you really missing out on? Strengthening your self-control builds character. Having the nerve to be different takes courage.

Tracking Data

But how do you compete with yourself every day? You do it by trying to beat your results from the day before, and the only way to do that is to keep score. Tracking your data creates that scorecard. Write down your current vertical jump. Write down your mile time. Know what you can currently do, then set a goal. Beat that goal. Set a new goal. Beat it, too.

If you never keep track or set goals, you are not learning how to compete. You are merely working out. Make everything you do a competition. That way, every rep has a purpose, and striving for more becomes your habit. If you are not willing to keep track of your results daily, you are not as dedicated as you should be.

Organize your data

Come up with a way to track your effort in an organized manner. Get a notebook, use a calendar, whatever works best, but find a way to log it, and keep this record with you. Keep track of what you do every day of the year—even if it is nothing. Seeing your daily effort and your days off is a powerful tool. Be faithful to this process, and eventually, it will become a habit. By the way, you will never outgrow the need to keep track of your progress, so spend as much time as you need figuring out an organized way to monitor it. It will be time well spent.

Show your results

It is important to show them to somebody. Peer pressure can be used to your advantage. There is more accountability when you know others will see your results. Again, if you were the only one who ever saw your report card, would you work as hard to earn good grades? Accountability is important.

Compete with yourself

If you want to get bigger, stronger, and faster, it is critical that you know how you performed your exercises yesterday. You should always be aiming for a number when competing with yourself. Always try to go up in something every day. If you add weight or add reps, you win, and these victories create a habit—a habit of winning. Some would call it an addiction. Be addicted to competing with yourself.

Be honest with yourself

The numbers don't lie. Be honest with yourself and with your current ability. Don't be the person who thinks they are faster than lightning, yet the numbers prove otherwise. The numbers are a measuring tool of your progress and will help you focus on striving for more. Along with functioning as your scorecard, you should consider them the grades of your sport. With that said, you should always know what your grades are at school. If you do not learn to compete with yourself, you will struggle and you will not reach your potential. Remember, coaches love a player who earns an academic scholarship.

Why would you not want to do this?

Two reasons: fear and laziness. When you compete with yourself every day, you also set yourself up to fail every day. Fear of failing on a daily basis can be difficult to deal with, and the fear of not being able to beat that number can cause you to stop keeping track. It will seem easier to be oblivious of your performance than to be sure of your failure. That is where the skill of competing comes in: knowing you may fail but trying your hardest not to is the sign of a true competitor.

Are you willing to do, both physically and mentally, what others are not? Your potential will be average if your effort is average. If you want to be elite, take what your coaches are telling you to do and double it. They are telling you what is needed to be average. Trust me, you cannot overhustle. Don't settle for average. Push the limits. Go extreme with your effort. There is no downside to it. Anything less is laziness.

According to Malcolm Gladwell in the book, *Outliers*[1], the difference between one student and another is what they do during the off-season. How they spend their summer puts them either ahead or behind other students at the beginning of the school year. During the school year, the students merely maintain that gap. It does not increase nor decrease, but the following summer, the gap increases even more.

With that in mind, if you want to create a gap between you and average, it must be done in the off-season. That means studying during the summer and training all year round. The greater the gap, the better the chance you will stand out and the more likely you are to receive a college scholarship. Baseball and school need to be a yearlong priority.

---

[1]Malcolm Gladwell, *Outliers*, (New York: Little, Brown and Company, 2008)

"Anything less than one hundred percent might as well be zero."

—Dr. Justin Wedding, orthodontist

7

The Physical Side

OK, so here is the chapter you have been waiting for. You may have even skipped the other chapters to get to this one. If you did that, please go back and read from the beginning. The concepts discussed are each built upon the one that preceded it—just like a strong technique. You cannot skip steps or chapters if you want to achieve a strong foundation.

If you have read every word to this point, good for you. You are well on your way to changing how you think. Now it is time to talk about the physical side of the student-athlete. In order to grow as a student or athlete, you must start at the most basic and build from there. Everything has a stage. This is most obvious with math. You begin by learning how to add, then subtract, then multiply, and then divide. If you do not have strong addition skills, you are going to struggle with every step that follows.

The same is true for sports. Your next step is built on the back of your current step. You must start with a strong foundation and reinforce it daily. You cannot skip steps. Good technique doesn't just happen. Embrace the process of going from a tricycle rider to one who competes in obstacle bike racing.

The first step is to be a student of the game. Always be learning something.

- Read
  Find books on technique. Read books written by great hitters or pitchers. Don't take every word as the truth, however. Be knowledgeable enough in the sport to understand if the concepts pertain to you.

- Watch videos
  Study the swings of players. Dissect them. Notice when their hips move. Know where they make contact. Track the path of the pitch. Did their swing match the plane of the pitch? Watch how a pitcher strides. When does their weight shift? Again, understand how their technique might pertain to you and how to implement it. For example, you may notice that most major league players stride when hitting, but also be sure to notice that the hitter's foot is planted long before his bat comes in contact with the ball.

- Watch games

    Try to focus on your position (or positions). Notice when and where they move with each pitch. Try and copy their ready stance. Watch their eyes when they catch the ball. You will see many of the fundamentals that you are learning still apply in the major leagues. That is not an accident. Fundamentals win games.

The second step is to not be a multitasker. Concentrate on one thing at a time. It is important to only think of the current pitch or the current class. Too much brain power is wasted on what doesn't matter. The last pitch is over. Think about the entire at bat once you are back in the dugout. Hitting a ball is difficult enough without your emotions hindering your focus. The same is true in the classroom. Don't stress about the next class and miss what needs to be learned in the current one.

Next is mental study. I know, you are thinking, "I thought we already covered the mental side of baseball," but I am talking about the mental visualization of the physical motions. This may sound obvious, but it needs to be said: you must think about and understand the knowledge that you gain before you can apply it. Before one repetition, understand what you must change and how you are going to change it. It will not come naturally. The old way is what has become natural. Think about it. If you cannot visualize the perfect swing, how do you expect to do one? You must see it in your mind's eye before your body can execute it.

"Hard work beats talent when talent doesn't work hard." That is one of my all-time favorite quotes, and it holds true. It isn't enough to be talented. You have to work hard.

What is talent anyway? According to *Merriam-Webster*, talent is "a special ability that allows someone to do something well." *Allows*, hmmm. This definition fits with the idea that talent is something that is a special prize that others have not received. Could that be? Maybe. Maybe they have been blessed with an extra large set of lungs or keen eyesight, but maybe they are physically normal and have developed their skills beyond the norm.

What if I told you that all talent comes from the brain? Tiny nerve endings fire away and create pathways. Could talent just mean that someone is a fast learner? Does that ruin the quote that I love? No, not at all. It actually confirms it. Just because one player learns a skill faster than another, he is labeled as talented, but that learning ability will slow down as the skills get harder. It is the diligent worker who prevails.

Understand that with every swing a memory pathway is either created or reinforced in your brain. When your brain has multiple equally thick pathways

72

to choose from and only one of them is correct, your odds of getting a good swing decreases. This is what causes inconsistency in a young athlete. On the other hand, if you continually reinforce a bad swing, it will have the thickest pathway and will most likely be the swing you see in a game. That is why precision and detail are so important. Not correcting a swing creates a deep pathway that is difficult to get out of. Think of a dirt road with deep ruts. Once your wheels slide into them, it is difficult to steer them out. To escape, you must start filling in those ruts by having a blueprint in your mind of what your swing should be. As you try to emulate that swing, stop as soon as your actions do not match your blueprint. Continue to do so until you have gone through the entire swing.

Learning is merely combining a bunch of small parts to create a whole. According to Daniel Coyle's book *The Talent Code*[2], this is called *chunking* and is the ticket to accelerated learning. He says that this is where talent is born—through detailed work.

Maybe you love learning because it comes easy, but maybe it comes easy because you love it and are willing to put in the work to achieve. Does it matter which one it is? All that matters is your willingness to do the work.

---

[2] Daniel Coyle, *The Talent Code: Greatness Isn't Born: Its Grown, Here's How*, (New York, Bantam Books, 2009)

How do you accomplish this accelerated learning?

Picture the perfect technique. Now picture yourself using the technique. Go slowly. Stop at multiple points to make sure you are imagining the perfect swing. This is difficult. Now, repeat, repeat, repeat. Get the message? Research shows "that mental practice—imagination, visualization, deep thought, and reflection—produces the same physical changes in the brain as would physically carrying out the same imagined processes."[3] Is that scary or exciting? It is scary if you cannot imagine a perfect technique and exciting if you can. Think of this mental image as programming your computer of a brain.

Now you are ready for mirror work. Mirror work is the slow-motion dissection of your swing and pitching strides. It is slow and tedious and may be the number one activity that separates a baseball player from someone who just plays baseball. It only takes a few minutes, but should be done every day. I cannot stress enough the importance of mirror work. Mirror work is the best way to deepen your memory pathways and increase your chances of obtaining the outcome you desire.

So if mentally thinking about the technique has the same effect as physically doing it, why physically

---

[3] Dr. Caroline Leaf, Switch On Your Brain, (Grand Rapids, MI, Baker Books, 2013), pg. 176

do mirror work? Why not just think it? Because thinking your muscle to move does not make them stronger. You still need to stand up and physically do the moves. Just make sure you are doing them properly before you start.

It is now time for some self-evaluation. Do you know what your swing looks like? Do you know what you need to work on? Ask someone to video your swing. Now ask someone to help you dissect it. This could be a coach or a parent, but seek someone who knows. Remember that change comes at a cost. It costs time and energy and often means you need a coach guiding you through the process.

Now go back to step one and start over.

I want to give you a few words about setbacks. Everyone has setbacks. Whether they are slumps or caused by an injury, you have the choice to view them as bad or as opportunities to grow. I like to think of them as a rubber band being pulled backward. They can end up being a way to fling yourself forward. Just realize that it takes time and much effort.

How we learn

Do not try to learn too much at one time. It is important to break down every fundamental into small building blocks. If you have ever built anything out of Legos, you know the wider and stronger the base, the higher the tower. Think of the fundamentals as the foundation, the base on which to build your skill. Now imagine the height of the tower is the level of baseball you end up playing. Trust me; you cannot spend too much time on the foundation.

Take the time to understand every little motion of your swing. Where are your hands? What are your feet doing? Where should your hips be? Shoulders? Head? You need to know these answers with every motion. Tedious but, if accurate, you will improve, and your foundation will become wider and stronger. Once you have programmed this technique into your brain, you can trust that you will perform it in a game and not have to think about it. That ultimately is the goal: know your technique, trust you know your technique, and let your body perform the technique.

I want to end this chapter with one last note. You must have the physique of a baseball player. For some, that means you need to lose weight, and for some, gain. Either way, to give yourself the best chance of playing baseball at a high level, you must develop agility and strength.

"It's the little details that are vital. Little things make big things happen."
— John Wooden, inducted in the Basketball Hall of Fame as both player and coach

8

Belief in Yourself

Many times we hear things like "believe in yourself"
or "you can do it if you set your mind to it." But what
do they mean? Do they mean that failure is caused by
your lack of belief or your inability to ignore your
insecurities? Honestly, that is too much pressure.
What if I said, "Believe in the process." Would that
make you feel less stress? How about "Honor where
you are, and learn from the process?" They are still
vague terms that can be interpreted many different
ways. How about "Be prepared"? Would that make
you feel like a Boy Scout? You know, there is a
reason that is their motto: it works. When you are
prepared, you have confidence. When you have
confidence, you have greater self-esteem. When you
have high self-esteem, you have a belief in yourself.

I know I said this book wasn't about motivation,
but this chapter will touch on it. I am not going to
give you a pep talk like a coach who is about to send

his players out onto the field, but rather, I am going to talk about a mind-set which will guide you through all your practices and games, not just the one at hand. This mind-set will also help you in school, and it goes well beyond a simple mental pep talk. It is a series of precise steps, which, if you have followed the plan to this point, you have already begun taking.

At this point, you should have written your mission statement and set many goals pertaining to school and athletics. You may have already achieved a few goals. If you have, you know you did not just hope your goals would be achieved. You took steps to make them happen. You must understand that being prepared is a process and not an instant fix.

Setting a goal—any goal—is the first step. The second is figuring out a way to achieve it. Sometimes that means you need to seek knowledge or guidance, but you cannot just sit there and hope change will occur. The third step is actually doing it.

Do not expect success with your first try. When you push yourself, you will fail. I watched a show on the female gymnasts training for the Olympics. They showed these talented young athletes trying over and over again to gain a new skill. They fell. They got back up. They fell again. That is what it takes. Eventually, they gained the skill, and then they began to reinforce it over and over again. They didn't stop because they finally got the skill right. They stopped when they no longer got it wrong. That is how you need to approach any skill:

- Decide on the skill to improve.
- Learn the correct process.
- Evaluate your current process.
- Break it down to small chunks.
- Feel the change from your current level.
- Practice it until you get it right.
- Practice it until you no longer get it wrong.
- Pick a new skill.

The fact that you wrote down a goal and took the necessary steps to achieve it tells me you believe you can do it. When you do the steps—even if you have yet to succeed—it shows me you believe. It should also show you. Prove to yourself you can achieve, and build on that. That, my friend, is how you build confidence, self-esteem, and ultimately, belief in yourself. You end up with a "been there, done that" attitude with a confidence brought on by experience. I know, not a magic formula or profound statement, but vital to any goal that you want to pursue.

If you are at all like me, when you feel unprepared, you become nervous. When I get nervous, my racing heart causes my brain to race. This causes the fight or flight hormones to take over. According to Wikipedia[4], the fight or flight response

---

[4] Wikipedia contributors, "Fight-or-flight response,"(*Wikipedia, The Free Encyclopedia,* 12 July 2016),

occurs when "the adrenal medulla produces a hormonal cascade that results in the secretion of catecholamines, especially norepinephrine and epinephrine. The hormones estrogen, testosterone, and cortisol, as well as the neurotransmitters dopamine and serotonin, also affect how organisms react to stress." I am not sure I know what all that means, but I am sure it isn't the environment I want when taking a test or trying to bat. Let's just agree that if you are prepared, there is much less stress, and knowing you are prepared when you walk onto a field or into a classroom will keep your focus on what is important.

If being prepared avoids stress, how do you prepare? In school, you study and pay attention in class. On the field, guess what? You study and pay attention. Know your plays. Know the signs. Those things are obvious. Less obvious is knowing what you are working on—in other words, your goals. Before every practice and every game, know what you are working on. It is just like a test at school. When you walk into the classroom, you should be familiar with the material covered on the test. It is obvious with school, not so much with sports. Make it just as obvious with sports. Know before the game that you will be working on squaring your hips or playing low to high. Though you have to execute many aspects of

https://en.wikipedia.org/w/index.php?title=Fight-or-flight_response&oldid=729460155

the game, pick three to five skills to focus on. The hard part will be sticking to them. So often players will revert back to their old habits because it is easier and they are less likely to commit an error, but stick with your goals. Be determined to be a better ballplayer after the game than you were before—regardless of the outcome. The skills will come if you stick to improving them.

So how do you know what to work on? One way is by daily journaling. This is different than tracking your workout stats. This is personal. These are your thoughts, and keeping a journal is a way to measure your mind-set and remind you of your goals.

When you journal, you will know if your attitude is where it should be and if you are honestly reinforcing a positive mind-set. I understand negative thoughts happen, and I think it is important to honor them, but do not let them catch you off guard. You must know when they are creeping into your head, because they will creep into your workouts and studying and, eventually, into your games and tests if you don't stop them. Think of negative thoughts as toxic to your attitude. If you ate poison, would you expect it to affect your body? Of course you would, but we "eat" mental poison daily. Healthy food creates a healthy body. The same is true with your mind-set. You need to encourage yourself along the way.

Be careful what you think about. In the book, *Switch On Your Brain*, Dr. Caroline Leaf writes, "If you say you can't or won't, this decision will actually cause protein synthesis and change in your brain into [sic] 'I can't' or 'I won't.'"[5] She also says, "If you don't get rid of a thought, you reinforce it." Your brain cannot distinguish between a thought and reality, and your muscles are controlled by your brain. As soon as you say, "I can't," you won't.

It is easy to understand the need to know your workout stats, but it is equally (if not more) important to know where you stand mentally. You need to know where you are both mentally and physically in order to stay positive. I know you hear that all the time, but it really does make a difference.

Try to surround yourself with positive people. I realize you cannot always control your environment, but you can learn to function on a high level, in spite of others wanting to bring you down. The surprising thing is that attitude is contagious. Be part of the solution instead of part of the problem. Your attitude will encourage others to join your positive side. I have found that one of the best ways to do that is by calling out the complainers in a positive way. Most don't realize they are complaining. If you learn to do that, you have gained another life skill. You have learned to be a leader.

Now about your parents. They really do have your best interests in mind. I realize there are exceptions, but in general, they want to see you succeed. Try to

---

[5] Leaf, *Switch On Your Brain*, Pg. 175

understand that they are grown up and understand how difficult your dream is to attain. Learn to communicate with them. Discuss what success means. Let them know when you are struggling. Consider them your accountability partners.

Belief in yourself is not always easy, and sometimes a little doubt can be a swift kick in the pants, but do not let it destroy you. Do not let it fester in your brain. Do not settle for where you are now, because your future holds as much improvement as your work ethic will allow.

"If I believe that I became the best quarterback that I could possibly be, the best football player that I could possibly be... That's how I'm going to measure my career as a success or not."

Tim Tebow, NFL football player

9

Character

Is good character necessary to make it in sports? You know the answer to that just by reading the headlines. But those same headlines also teach us that a strong character is necessary for success in life, in spite of the fact that it is a rare commodity. According to the *Huffington Post* in an article from February 20, 2014, 75 percent of college students admit to cheating[6]. Does that make it right?

Following is a list of the keys to a strong character. Read all of them and focus on one or two at a time to make them a habit. Then concentrate on two more until all of them become your way of life. This isn't baseball, and yet, it is. These characteristics will

---

[6] Bryce Buchmann, "Cheating In College: Where It Happens, Why Students Do it, and How to Stop It," Huffington Post, February 20, 2014)
http://www.huffingtonpost.com/uloop/cheating-in-college-where_b_4826136.html

help you get recruited and, more importantly, make you grow as an individual.

These keys are important in the classroom as well as on the field.

- **Want success for others**
  Be glad when your classmates earn recognition. Do not envy their praise, and never view their praise as a slight on you. The same goes for teammates. Be genuinely happy for their success. Learn from it, and be glad you have a role model.

- **Be grateful**
  Realize that you are one of the lucky ones. You get to practice and play baseball and attend school. You are on a journey of knowledge and skill, both of which are important for your future. I know that sounds preachy, but you will be surprised how much faster and how much more you learn with that type of attitude. You may also be surprised at how contagious that attitude is.

- **Accept where you are while striving for more**
  Understand that academics as well as sports are processes. The next step is built on the current one. Be realistic with where you are, and do not skip steps or get frustrated if your progression isn't as fast as you hoped it would be. It will come

if you do not give up and if you stick with the plan.

- **Know that goals take time to achieve**

Instant isn't a reality. You did not learn to read in a day, and a good bat swing takes reps. Lots and lots of reps. The same is true for math and English. They take time to understand. This key is similar to the previous one. Everything worthwhile has a process, and you must be patient while going through it.

- **Understand that everyone has a different process**

Do not compare where you are with others. Do not let them hinder your process, and by all means, do not hinder theirs. Do not be disruptive in class or during practice. Remember: everyone learns differently and is at a different point in their process.

- **Be kind to your teammates no matter what their ability**

Have you seen the movie *Rudy*? If you have, you will understand what I am saying here. If you haven't seen it, you should. It is a perfect example of how a player can be invaluable to a team without playing in a game. Rudy was not an asset on the football field, but he contributed greatly to the team with his determination and refusal to quit. Be like Rudy and, for that matter, his teammates. They valued him. They treated him with respect. Be a benefit to your team beyond your athletic ability. Practice with heart, and encourage others to do the same, no matter what their skill level. Have the same attitude in the classroom. The goal for both the field and the classroom is a positive learning environment. That is achieved through respect and kindness.

- **Don't throw your teammates under the bus**
Never deflect blame on a teammate. You are in it together. Loyalty is vital. Let your teammates know you have their back. Hopefully, they will also have yours.

- **Correct your teammates or classmates with the purpose of helping**
Do not condemn or criticize others, but rather, help them achieve more. Speak in a respectful manner while you correct poor execution. You may find, in some instances, that a coach or teacher will not want you correcting anyone. That is fine. Respect your coach, but never tease or criticize a player. At the same time, accept correction from your teammates. If you don't believe the correction, ask your coach, but thank your teammate for taking the time to help you.

- **Don't be a draining complainer**

I am sure you know the kind of person I am talking about. No matter what the circumstance, they will complain. Don't be that guy. They drain the team of energy and focus. If you feel you have something to complain about, keep it to yourself, or better yet, try to improve the situation.

- **Seek out opportunities to encourage**

It is amazing what a few positive words can do for someone. Everyone needs encouragement from time to time. Look for those times.

It should be obvious that everything on this list is under your control. They are all choices that, when practiced, will become a habit. The bottom line to character is self-control. Nothing destroys chemistry on a team like a fit. Self-control is one of the keys to a successful life. It is what keeps you staying the course instead of quitting.

"Do you want to know who you are? Don't ask. Act! Action will delineate and define you."

Thomas Jefferson, Founding Father of The United States of America

10

Road Blocks and Detours

Keys to Staying the Course

This chapter will be the hardest by far to stick to. Up to now, everything has been presented in individual steps. Now comes the time when you have to put them together every day. It is easy to stay motivated for a day or even a week, but month after month and year after year is a different story. So many times you will wonder why you are putting so much effort into a dream. So many times you will want to slack off or even quit. I am not saying you have to be obsessed with school and baseball, but I am saying you have to be dedicated.

What is your weakness? Everyone has one. Do you know the story of Achilles's heel? The short version is that Achilles was a Greek hero who was invincible except for his heel. His strength was unlike any other, but the weakness of his heel was his undoing. What is your Achilles heel? Is it time with friends, video games, insecurity? Understand that everyone has a weakness, but realizing what it is will help keep it from destroying your dream.

Find your weakness. Label it. Understand what triggers it. Make it a part of your mission statement and then read your mission statement daily— especially when you don't want to. It will help remind you of why you are working so hard.

Next, keep your eyes open for roadblocks and curves in the road. There are many excuses for veering off your path. Looking for them will help keep them at bay and possibly eliminate their threat. I will describe some of the potential roadblocks and even dead ends, but it is your job to recognize them in your life.

I believe the most common is **fear**. There are many kinds of fear, but one is fear of being laughed at. Admitting you want to play college baseball will garner strange looks and disbelief. Hopefully by now you know it won't be easy, but it isn't impossible. Being mocked is an instant deflator. Stick to your dreams. Keep climbing your mountain.

Sometimes the fear comes from within. Perhaps, at some point, you will doubt you have what it takes. That is normal. It comes with self-evaluation, but instead of letting it defeat you, let it fuel your desire to work harder. Many star athletes weren't good enough to make teams growing up, but it made them work even harder. I wonder how many talented athletes chose to quit instead of rising to the challenge? Did you know that J. J. Watt was a walk-on at Wisconsin?

There may come a time when you begin to doubt the work is worth the cost. Being dedicated takes sacrifice, but the rewards of learning how to be dedicated far outweigh the temporary cost. You are learning a lifelong skill. Dedication is a muscle that needs to be strengthened. It is not something you are born with.

I think the hardest fear to overcome is the fear of the process. When you doubt the way to achieve your goals, you begin to waffle, and then you lose much of your drive. When your path isn't clear, you go in circles. I watched a *MythBusters* episode the other day. Adam and Jamie were blindfolded and had their ears covered, and the only task they had to do was walk a straight line. They couldn't do it. It was comical how bad they were at it. It seemed so easy, but apparently, it is not. You will be bad at it, too, if you try to reach a goal when you can no longer see where you are going, and you no longer believe what you hear—whether that is from your coach or your own head. Keep studying and seeking knowledge. That is the only way you will be able to believe in the process.

Another major setback is **loss of drive**. When you convince yourself your goal is no longer important, it is difficult to find your drive—some would say it is impossible. You must regain your belief in your goal's importance, or your progress will be terminally slowed. With that in mind, remember the saying "a knife is easy to dull." It means that your desire (the knife) is squelched (dulled) when progress is slower than expected. It takes time to get better at anything. The hard part is the better you get at baseball, the more difficult it is to improve and the longer it takes. The progress continues to slow until it is creeping so slowly that it is hardly visible. You must learn to trust that improvement is happening. I've got news for you: most want to improve, but few are willing to put in the necessary work. It is the ability to get beyond the instant gratification of success that is the difference between being diligent and being passive, being great and being average.

The less obvious roadblocks are the many **diversions** that occur in life. Wanting to spend time on other things is normal, but I was under the impression you wanted to be more than normal. Why else would you be reading this book? Let me remind you of the quote "Anything not worth doing is not worth doing well." Remember that one. I love that quote, and honestly, it has changed how I spend some of my free time. Don't spend your time getting good at something that doesn't matter. (I am not talking about algebra, however.)

Another less obvious road block is **arrogance**. When you believe you no longer have to work hard because you are good enough, I call that arrogance. If the pros continue to work on their craft, never believe you have mastered your skills. That is arrogant laziness—too good to work hard. There is always more to learn.

That leads to something that may be hard to understand, but possibly the biggest dream killer. Sometimes being **recognized as great** can be your greatest downfall. Believing you are better than others can slow your progress, not just because you may become arrogant but because you become afraid to change anything that you do. It is easy to want to change your swing if you are not having success. It is difficult when you are having success. Putting it another way, a home run is pointless if your swing is flawed, but your fear of not hitting a home run may keep your swing in its flawed form. Sometimes it is difficult to look at the big picture, but that is what you have to do to have the guts to change.

Which, believe it or not, is connected to the next road block, **loss of confidence**. Once you lose confidence, it is difficult to get it back. Recognize what can zap your confidence. If you are results oriented, you will lose confidence whenever you have a bad game. Realize you will make mistakes, have a poor performance, have a bad day. Realize there will be times when you won't be able to do what others can do.

Hitting is probably one of the biggest areas in which players lose confidence. Do not get caught up in the results. Does your batting average matter? No. It doesn't tell the whole story, and it is subjective. Let's face it, some pitchers are easier to hit than others, and some leagues are tougher than others. There is cause and effect in play here. If you focus on what matters, you will improve. If you focus on your batting average, you won't. Don't worry about that number. Doesn't that take the pressure off? Trust me, the better your swing plane, the more likely you are to get a hit. You will face tough pitchers, and you will have bad umpires, but your swing plane is something you can control and is what really matters. At the same time, the biggest mistake you can make is to think you are a great batter because you have a high batting average and another is discounting the importance of a great swing.

Prepare. Bad days happen. It is not the end of the world. If you didn't prepare, that is different. If you give 100 percent and you strike out twice, understand it happens. Never change your fundamentals because of a couple at bats, and never think about the batting order. If the order is changed, don't panic and put undue pressure on yourself. The most important hitter is the one in the batter's box.

It is important to be relaxed, comfortable, and hardworking. Be the hardest-working guy on the team. Don't be results oriented, or you may change your swing just to get a hit. Understand you have a role, and just do your best. And one last word: never bat to make contact. Oh, one more word: read your mission statement daily.

"Nothing can stop the man with the right mental attitude from achieving his goal; nothing on earth can help the man with the wrong mental attitude."

—Thomas Jefferson, Founding Father of The United States of America

11

Conclusion

Minimal effort brings minimal results. Maximum effort brings maximum results. There is a direct correlation between effort and results that cannot be reasoned away or, more importantly, absolved through excuses. Your results are your own, and they begin with your mind-set. If you want to just get by all your life, do the minimum. But I ask you, why limit yourself?

When you choose the path, either athletically or academically, and you do not do the work but you tell everyone you do, at some point it will catch up with you. You will know when you look in the mirror. You have but one shot. You cannot get a do-over. Are you giving it your best shot? Will you give it your best shot? For the rest of your life, you will have to live with yourself knowing the truth.

I talk a lot about what matters and what doesn't, and at times it may seem like they conflict, but they don't. What level you are at right now does not determine or guarantee any form of success or lack thereof. At the same time, you have to know where you are right now in order to determine your strengths and weaknesses and create a pathway to your goals.

Your ability to hit a home run means nothing if your swing is flawed. Your ability to hit a home run will end when the pitching catches up with you, but if your fundamentals are strong, they will carry you to the next level. It is imperative that you know the difference between basic skill and pure strength. You will experience at some time in your sport life the chasm between the boys who hit puberty early and those who hit it late. The early bloomers will dominate the sport until the others catch up. The downfall for the early bloomers is that they tend to rely more on their strength than on the basics, and those who are late bloomers tend to lose heart. Don't get caught up in that. Keep working on your skills— no matter where you lie in the puberty time line. Never rely on your strength, but let your strength enhance your game—whenever your strength comes.

Tony Gwynn was inducted into the Baseball Hall of Fame in 2007. He is considered one of the best and most consistent hitters in baseball history, but when he was in a slump, he went down to the minors to watch the batters. He tried to figure out what they were doing right. He was trying to figure out what bad habits he had acquired that were affecting his batting average. I find that amazing and a good lesson. No one is above learning.

You have to decide, not your parents or coaches, if you want to be successful at this. Decide your mission. Own your goal. Make that choice, and accept that every practice matters, and every class matters. Have the mind-set that you are going to push yourself in everything you do. Between classes and between workouts, you can be a kid, but during school and during practice, be focused on what you are doing and only that. Do not be distracted when it is time to work. Make your work ethic a daily habit.

People are going to try to veer you off your path. If you choose to listen to them, you will not accomplish your goals. How many of your friends will be with you in college? Do not put your friends above your goals. Find friends who have similar goals.

Please realize your baseball career could be over in a heartbeat, but the lessons learned in becoming a scholar-athlete will last you a lifetime. Do not take these lessons lightly; they will mold your future.

"If the ax is dull and it edge unsharpened, more strength is needed, but skill will bring success."
Ecclesiastes 10:10

Form for Success

What is your path?
Academically:

_____

_____

Athletically:

_____

_____

What are the pros and cons of your academic path?
Pros:

_____

_____

_____

Cons:

_____

_____

_____

What are the pros and cons of your athletic path?
Pros:

_____

_____

_____

Cons:

_____

_____

_____

Dream school?

_____

Name three of their academic scholarship?

_____

_____

_____

Name of their baseball stadium?

_____

Who is their current coach?

_____

How will you achieve your path?
Academically:

_____

_____

_____

_____

_____

Athletically:

_____

_____

_____

_____

_____

How much time are you willing to invest after school towards your goals?

Day	Academic	Athletic	Personal
Monday			
Tuesday			
Wednesday			
Thursday			
Friday			
Saturday			
Sunday			

Note: Please be realistic and put time in minutes.

Who will hold you accountable?

_____

_____

_____

Have you asked all of them to hold you accountable?

Y   N

What are your goals?
Academic 5 year:

_____

_____

_____

Athletic 5 year:

_____

_____

_____

Academic 1 year:

_____

_____

_____

Athletic 1 year:

_____

_____

_____

Personal 5 year:

_____

_____

_____

Personal 1 year:

_____

_____

_____

What are your strengths?
Academically:

_____

_____

_____

Athletically:

_____

_____

_____

Personality:

_____

_____

_____

What are your weaknesses?
Academically:

_____

_____

_____

Athletically:

_____

_____

_____

Personality:

_____

_____

_____

List your closest friends and next to their name write down if that person is supportive or tends to distract you from your mission and goals:

Name	Supportive or Distraction

List your most time consuming activities and next to them write down if the activity helps or hurts your success in achieving your goals:

Activity	Helps or Hurts

What are you willing to sacrifice in order to reach your goals?

_____

_____

_____

_____

_____

_____

_____

_____

What could cause you to not reach your goal?

Academically:

_____

_____

_____

Athletically:

_____

_____

_____

Personally:

_____

_____

_____

_____

The Guy in the Glass
by Dale Wimbrow, (c) 1934

When you get what you want in your struggle for pelf,
And the world makes you King for a day,
Then go to the mirror and look at yourself,
And see what that guy has to say.

For it isn't your Father, or Mother, or Wife,
Who judgement upon you must pass.
The feller whose verdict counts most in your life
Is the guy staring back from the glass.

He's the feller to please, never mind all the rest,
For he's with you clear up to the end,
And you've passed your most dangerous, difficult test
If the guy in the glass is your friend.

You may be like Jack Horner and "chisel" a plum,
And think you're a wonderful guy,
But the man in the glass says you're only a bum
If you can't look him straight in the eye.

You can fool the whole world down the pathway of years,
And get pats on the back as you pass,
But your final reward will be heartaches and tears
If you've cheated the guy in the glass.

Bibliography

Daniel Coyle, *The Talent Code: Greatness Isn't Born: Its Grown, Here's How*, (New York, Bantam Books, 2009)

Malcolm Gladwell, *Outliers*, (New York: Little, Brown and Company, 2008)

Dr. Caroline Leaf, Switch On Your Brain, (Grand Rapids, MI, Baker Books, 2013)

"The Guy in the Glass" (used by permissions by Peter Dale Wimbrow, Jr. as a grateful memory of his father, the author, Dale Wimbrow 1895-1954

Online:

Wikipedia contributors, "Fight-or-flight response,"(*Wikipedia, The Free Encyclopedia,* 12 July 2016), https://en.wikipedia.org/w/index.php?title=Fight-or-flight_response&oldid=729460155

Bryce Buchmann, "Cheating In College: Where It Happens, Why Students Do it, and How to Stop It," Huffington Post, February 20, 2014) http://www.huffingtonpost.com/uloop/cheating-in-college-where_b_4826136.html

About the Authors

Gary McDonald is the president of D1 Mentality in Las Vegas, Nevada, where he is developing student-athletes nationally who go on to reach their potential academically and athletically. Prior to starting D1 Mentality, Gary was an athletic director, educator, and coach. His past student-athletes have gone on to all five power conferences and numerous other programs.

Gary has a wife, Kelly, three children, Travis, Kayli, and Ryan, and a dog named Scout. Ryan currently plays baseball for West Virginia University. Gary also has two grandchildren, Hadlee and Hudson.

Melody Forrest is a mother of three and a grandmother of two. Her youngest son, Scott, has been coached by Gary for many years, and watching him share his knowledge with his players through the years made Melody want to share that knowledge with every future adult.

Melody is currently working on *The Fairy Tale Trilogy* and expects the first of the series, *Maid to Perfection*, to be released in late 2016.